Waiting for the Light
to Change

Waiting for the Light to Change

Poems by Bernadette McBride

Word Press

© 2013 by Bernadette McBride

Published by Word Press
P.O. Box 541106
Cincinnati, OH 45254-1106

ISBN: 9781625490261
LCCN: 2013908201

Cover art: Andrew Reynolds Duffy
Author photo: Dino Sanchez

Poetry Editor: Kevin Walzer
Business Editor: Lori Jareo

Visit us on the web at www.word-press.com

Acknowledgments

I am grateful to the editors of the following publications where these poems, some in slightly altered form, first appeared:

Cider Press Review: "A Blight in the Growing Season"
Freshet: "Lesson"
Ibbetson Street Press: "Storm," "When Our Guests Have Gone," "Intersection," "Good Friday"
The Penwood Review: "The Angelus," "Contemplating Constance Charpentier's Melancholy"
Schuylkill Valley Journal: "Miscarriage," "The Leaving," "Bronze Veins," "To Old Women"
St. Joseph's University Magazine: "On a March Morning"
US 1 Worksheets: "Knowing Early What Others Have Lately Known," "Life for the Real Artist"
Waukegan Public Library Online: "Bride of Christ"

"Bride of Christ" won Second Place for the annual international Ray Bradbury Writing Award in 2006.

"Mother" appeared in making *Magic: Beauty in Word and Image* (November 2012-March 2013) exhibit at the Michener Museum, Doylestown, PA.

I also offer my deepest thanks to Christopher Bursk, master poet, mentor, and friend, for his steady guidance, along with George Drew and Marie Kane—all lent their skill and generosity of time and wisdom to help craft the final manuscript of this book; to April Lindner for her invaluable counsel, to Sandra Becker, Laura Holloway, Paula Raimondo, and Wendy Steginsky for their always-reliable insight and good humor; to Katherine Falk, Israel Halpern, Allen and Debi Hoey, Susan B. Katz, Herb and Pamela Perkins-Frederick, and Bill Wunder for their encouragement; to Tenaya Darlington, Melissa Goldthwaite, and Ann Green for their help and suggestions; to the Bucks County poetry community for their collective and constant support, and to those remarkable fellow poets who read individual poems along the way to forming this collection.

Thank you, always, to my husband, Andrew Reynolds Duffy, for sharing with me the gifts of his clear perspective, musical ear, and patience, and to my children, Monica and Michael, for their abiding inspiration.

For Andy, Monica, and Michael
and for my parents, Cleat and Miriam

Where the spirit does not work with the hand, there is no art.
—Leonardo da Vinci

Table of Contents

I.

Planting Alone 15
Interior 16
Knowing Early What Others Have Lately Known 17
Thursday Was Rubbish Day 18
To Old Women 19
The Angelus 20
Mallo Cups 21
The Finer the Neighborhood, the Fewer People Are About 22
Flying Lessons 23
Boreas 24
Chica in a Bar 26
Slow Motion 27
The Lady of Shalott 28

II

Intersection 33
Of a Young Man Dying 34
Still, in Your 17th Year 37
21st Century Musings on a 17th Century Child 38
Good Friday 39
Circuition 40
Hail the Horse 43
Saturdays 44
On Johannes Vermeer's *The Milkmaid* 45
Small Things 46
The Same Sunset 47
April Buck 49

III

Spoil of War 53
Bronze Veins 57
The Potato Eaters 58
Miscarriage 59
On a March Morning 60
Lesson 61
Storm 62
A Slight Remove 63
A Blight in the Growing Season 64
Carried Cups of Tea 66

On Receiving News of Sudden Death 67
Stuck in the Thick 68
The Leaving 69
Offering Grace 70
Contemplating Constance Charpentier's *Melancholy* 71
Taking Away the Keys 72
Thrift Shop 74
Madame X 75
Still Life on a Buffet 76
When Our Guests Have Gone 77

IV
Mother 81
Bride of Christ 82
The Saint of Calcutta 83
Life for the Real Artist 84
An Artist Becoming 85
Make Me Believe 90

I

Planting Alone

White sky of July morning. The heat
pricks through the weave of her broad boater,
draws sweat along each strand of hair to pool
in the hat band, seep down through eyelashes

she swipes with her dirty cuff, its broken button
catching at the corner of her eye, drawing tears
to blur her vision. No matter. She's on a mission.

Her dirty, ovaled fingernails turn rainbow
up close in full sun, remind her
why she kneels here—the lush of cool soil
between her fingers, the dark damp, a release.

At the edge of her petaled beds, she plants
new vinca, pink and white—deterrents
to the deer who appear each morning to lick

the salt block, keep their daylight distance,
having scavenged overnight each effort she's made
with impatiens and pansy, tulip and zinnia,
toward beauty in this desperate garden.

Interior
        —Peter Vilhelm Ilsted, 1896

Why is the tiny clock placed so high on the wall,
so distant from the life of the setting? The muted
girl, her smooth jug in hand, stands fixed, far,
in her silence, from the tick of time, the rush
of endeavor beyond this halved room. Hutch,
dress, table cover cluster—lit by the window's
thin shaft that hush-dapples each object in its
scope—evoke as much question as response.
Where did Ilsted desire our eye to roam?
To her? To the tabled glass bottle from which
his blue diffuses? Or did he purposely brush in
the clock with its weight in the negative space
of the painting—a reminder of the human hold
which defines everything framed.

Knowing Early What Others Have Lately Known
—after William B. and Emily

She was ten the first time she pretended
to be dead, lying in the center of her bed
holding her breath—over her heart, her hands
folded, fixed with a Kleenex lily. She listened
for the sobbing, pictured her family passing,
her friend, Patricia, Sister Mary Madeline,
and Thomas, the boy who'd laughed at her
Valentine card. Listened for their laments,
hoping. But heard only the bee-loud breeze
outside the screened window. Within, a blue,
uncertain, stumbling buzz. When, at last, her mother
called her down to lunch, she jumped, crumpled
the lily to her pocket, and raced downstairs
to drink her milk, and will away her hunger.

Thursday Was Rubbish Day

Sizzling asphalt glinted sticky in the humid morning,
sucked at our sneaker soles as we waited

quiet, lining the curb, leaning in a collective squint
that pierced the haze; yearned toward the labored approach

of the four-wheeled dragon as it rumbled and roared from block
to city block. A steel behemoth, big-jawed, crunching,

it advanced, gulping the neighborhood's waste heaped
in dented silver barrels left and right—hand-fed

by filthy-gloved, muscled men with smeared faces,
sweat dripping through soot, trickling to the corners

of cigaretted mouths that promised us the next wave—
the water truck—that giant tortoise emerged, still dripping

from the city reservoir. We chased the cool slashes clear into
the next block, the lovely sooty spray splattering bare calves,

blackening ankle socks as we, in unbound glee,
leapt and whooped in the exquisite itch of summer.

To Old Women
    —for Margaret Gatley McBride

As they watch from soft green porches,
low sun slanting across urn-potted geraniums,
the neighbor women bustle by,

handbags swagged over dimpled elbows,
sturdy shoes treading the root-raised sidewalk
of the old block where the 4 o'clock ping

of green beans snapped to the waiting pot
—their cool smell in summer—
begins the close of day.

To their flowered house dresses and girdles,
their pointy-cornered bifocals, blue-permed hair,
and Coty-ed mouths smiling

from Kodak shots taken at abundant tables.
To their waiting for letters from daughters and sons
at war, lips tight, their titanium refusal

to believe in anything less than hope.
To the slip of a dollar to a grandchild's palm,
the scent of Camay in the white-tiled bath,

and the Sunday dinners carried
dish by dish from steaming yellow kitchens
to double-leafed tables. To the funeral luncheons,

the grey-day placings of cut flowers at the tombs,
the vast ache of wakings-up and lyings-down,
and the prayers. All the prayers.

To all of these. Amen. Amen.

The Angelus
        —Jean-Francois Millet, 1857

Note the distant spire, almost missed
on first viewing, and though the canvas

can be only seen and felt, not heard,
we know the bell tolls, rolls its beckon

across the wheat and wind, prompts
the reverence of this man, this woman

of the land, their humble pause at the close
of day: bowed heads, halted hands,

sweating brows planed by thanks
vaulting like the glide of birds above them

in the parted clouds. Their work honored
by healthy crops. Their rest earned,

burned in a tradition now all but gone,
revered here. The glean of God and man merged,

its richness rendered in these amber tones
that extol the soil, the light, which yield.

Mallo Cups

They arrived as a brown-paper cube
tied with string gone greasy with transport
which on removal, showed them glowing
sun-like in red and yellow paper tucked neat

like teeth in the ordered space. I lifted one out
to eat and rushed the rest to the freezer, smacked
with a Scotch-taped sign: *All Mine*. I had, after all,
been the one who'd every day for months bought

with recess money one little square at Silverman's
on the way home from school. The one who'd saved,
according to directions, the collection of cardboard
play money flatted under the brown accordioned cups

in each wrapped package. The one who'd counted
and traded almost daily the 10- and 25-cent coupons
for 5 eventual $1 cards, all that was needed to send
for them. And the one who'd waited for weeks

for the prize to arrive, for the proof all this work
had not been in vain. So, to my 5th-grade way
of thinking they warranted my reasoning,
my hoarding. My first fling at strategized greed.

The Finer the Neighborhood, the Fewer People Are About
(line from Carson McCullers' The Member of the Wedding)

But, oh, the thick
of town, the mess,
the luxurious annoyances.
The lure of neon energy
and those bits
of melted tar—
black chewing gum
glittered in the sun—
easy-peeled like sunburned
skin between forefinger
and thumb.
The side streets full
of the cracking of bats,
the *tock* of the ball;
the crowded smell
of bus exhaust,
frying onions,
thick-air sticky—
more pungent
than warm hay,
than the pleasure
of a long whiff of your
own sweaty hair;
tart as lit punks
in evening,
their swirling incense
twirling torch-orange
figure-eights
through the dark.
And those shouts of kids
cupping lightning bugs
the second they show.

Flying Lessons

We'd hide in those years, Kate and I, behind the last station
in the Bio lab—sneaking down from our dorm room, certain

Sister Andrea didn't know. Smoking Salems, we giggled
above the slant of a copped flashlight shrunk to Lady Chatterly

and John Thomas spirited from the nuns' private library
where we smiled our way by dust cloths and Pledge.

We lived as sheltered vagabonds then, roaming the convent halls
in curlers and bunny slippers, dipping out of sight at the swish

of habit skirts, the click of rosary beads: the bed-check patrol
we sidetracked with puffed-up pillows buried beneath blankets

in the low glow of a Virgin Mary night light. Our days opened
and shut like the hard-backed books we lugged around

in drawstring sacks from class to class, skimming their surfaces
like fledglings dipping at the skin of a lake. Only half mindful

of the lessons electric in the passion of our teachers, half alert
to the gaining weight of our widening minds.

Boreas

—J.W. Waterhouse, 1902

Romance fans
down
the center
of the canvas:
the pink triangle

of cheek-elbow-hand,
the sprinkled pink
of sky,
of blossom,

her dappled
left shoulder,
the drape
of her shawl.

What swoop
and swirl,
what lush,
what pensive purple!

So North,
so slate,
so lavish
in movement!

Such lure,
such situation
in time,
in mind!

What else
but to drink
in one
long
plummed
swallow.

Chica in a Bar
—Ramon Casas, 1892

*I told him I'd be wearing red
and would take a table under the mirror*

*(he'll notice this way the sweep of my hair
at the back as well).*

*I know how to lure un hombre, oh, si.
I had thought he'd use that center door*

*since he'd be coming from...wait, is that...?
No. Just when I am thinking* this one

would be the other *I could depend on—
all those sidelong smiles as I passed him*

*loading shrimp to the dock, those
golden shoulders browned*

*as the distant mountains; the sincerity
in his serenades from the pavement*

*at the edge of the water. Perhaps he has,
eh—how you say—cold feet? Or, someone*

*warned him I'm really a lady
behind these scarlet lips?*

*Or...merda! Perhaps he spotted
this lit cigar before* I *spotted* him.

Slow Motion

That summer, we were the exhausting charges of our guardian angels,
mostly in those back-and-forth midnight drives across the bay bridge
on our way to *The Attic*. We watched the uniform lines of mainland lights

streak some old comfort across the dark water as we drove too fast,
cheeks flushed by the salt-wind blowing in through the open windows
of the banged-up Buick, restless for the rush of the Club's

after-hours band who worked hard and well at Chicago's "Beginnings"
and "Does Anybody Really Know What Time It Is?" The black walls
and black lights emphasized the implications of white papier-mâché

Venus de Milos locking eyes with milky *Davids* set on pedestals
arched above our heads as we tumbled in under the setting moon—
our tides of hair and bell-bottoms and halter tops drenched in the scent

of salt air and shellfish, our chests swelled with anticipation
heightened by all those backseat roaches and passed-around Millers.
We flowed in slow motion, bewitched till dawn by long-haired,

love-beaded loves. Then turned back across the water with the sun,
to sink to, reach for, oblivion, wake late to another of an endless string
of beach days laden with languor and lust and put-off duty.

The Lady of Shalott
—J.W. Waterhouse, after poem by Alfred, Lord Tennyson
(a muse on the artist's plan)

I shall place her in her dark boat
at the brink of launch—forlorn, comely,
flanked by the flit of two birds—

ensconced with what means most to her.
Her embroidered quilt with its portraits
of her longings will cushion the wooden seat

as it drapes over the reeds, muting
their sharp crackle as she glides, fading.
It will mimic the downward pull of willows

that weep silent, dry, as does she.
Her left hand will fold toward
her empty womb, allow gazers

their own conclusions as to whom each
lies open; the right will control
the chain that has kept her captive

in the half-life that prompts at last
this final journey—the life whose purity
a white dress will reflect. Her lips,

auburn, parted as if to sigh,
will match the veil of hair that bespeaks
both romance and her nun-like seclusion,

their hues mirrored in the foliage
that will heat the distant glade.
One tall candle's light will battle the breeze,

winning (two more, like thieves, extinguished),
keeping vigil for a shrine to a beads-bound
crucified Christ—a reflection

of her own anguish at the elusive Lancelot—
unbeknownst—haunting, luring her,
my dear, ill-starred Lady of Shalott.

II

Intersection

An old man in a worn red parka lingers
in the north yard of the church

on the corner of 2nd and Main, his back
to the grit of traffic as he bows

toward a new-flowered tomb—modest
among an assembly of angels

made of stone. I watch him from my place
in the line of cars waiting for the light

to change. His white hair lifts in the wind,
thin strands standing upright, brushing pale

against a scrim of low, gathering clouds—
a feathery crown yearning toward heaven.

He is fixed in an invisible cocoon, wings
still curled; reverent hands folded

one over the other—chapeled away from us,
who, when the light goes green, will continue

to compete our ways home. Most
to be greeted by the living.

Of a Young Man Dying
    —for Alex, my son's best friend

I
Clean, they said—
no drink, no drugs
just an urgency
of youth the fault

they said

he never knew
what hit him—that he
knew no pain, the force
of the crash
having been so great,
the railroad gate's

having approached
like a meteor—unavoidable
by this late swerve.

But what do they know—
the knowing so sudden:

the wide eyes
the clutch
at the heart
the pulse
the prayer

the silent wheel
unspun.

II
I smooth your flyaway hair, long, blue-black, ice-cold. Study
the talc-lidded eyes that could see the rainbow in beads of sweat,

the purple in winter trees. I mourn the whitened lips
whose movement you reserved for kindness, for humor; trace

the First-Communion rosary weaving your fingers.
And here is Michael's Phillies hat—the one you begged him for—

the one he wouldn't give up (*No, man! It's brand new!*)
—going with you now. I recall the time he told me

about the skateboard incident in Love Park—your first year
in Art school, living on your own in the city—when those punks

punched you in the face; broke your glasses
because you wouldn't turn over your cool board to them—

you, peaceful as the Buddha, bent on not fighting back.
And that winter night you had dinner with us when you visited

from Portland and Michael was working—I apologized
for the sticky rice and you said, "No worries, my dad always makes

sticky rice at home," a nod to the Japanese half of your heritage.
We laughed and passed around the fish. Now, I kneel here

and think about your heart, your lungs, your brain, all intact still.
But this cold: how can we who are left question the soul's fire?

III
The boys stand in a circle in the vestibule, toes pointing
to the empty center, Alex's father the linchpin.
Tell us again what happened, and they shift their Nikes,
Sketchers, Docs from left to right to left as they listen.
Yes, he'd had on his seat belt. No, he hadn't been drinking.
Yes, the two who had been with him walked away with scratches.
No, he felt no pain, death was instantaneous.

The boys ask again, gulping, trying to smile at family members
arriving. They go back to the open casket again, again, as though
maybe this time he'll sit up, remind them, *No worries*.
They hug each other, hug his mother, stare back at the blue-black hair,
some flyaway strands making a halo. At the appointed time,
they circle the casket, lift together, reverence their friend from altar
to hearse to burial, their twelve sturdy shoes facing forward,
Alex's, toward the stars.

Still, in Your 17th Year

Once you're asleep, I switch off your light
and bless you with the sacraments left to me—

Reiki hands and artless intentions,
my thumb making the sign of the cross

on your forehead. I summon the angels,
tall, big-winged, to line the walls

of your room; stand guard against your fears,
your doubts about joy past this new loss.

Once, you woke, rubbing your eyes—
disbelieving—asking me why I treat you

like a baby, when I know you're not sure
now prayer has ever worked.

The drone of ritual in time stripped away
the mystery that made you wide-eyed

when, long ago, outside the church,
that old man gave you a dollar—

just after you'd worried to the collection plate
the one I had tucked to your tiny hand.

You asked me if he was God.

21st Century Musings on a 17th Century Child
    —on *Prince Felipe Prospero* by Diego Velazquez, 1659

For how long did he stand like this, fighting the boyish
urge to wiggle, to dash to lighter, windowed rooms?
The dark-eyed gaze that pierces ours from the pallor
of his tiny face reflects this bleak hall where he waits,
bedecked in charms, an amulet, one silver bell—
cord-strung across his chest, around his waist—placed
to repel the threats bounding toward him—the feared end
of his family's glory by his own imminent death,
their hopes for him fading like the little languid hand draped
in fatigue over the back of his velvet chair. And still, he
holds; stares as though imploring us to pluck him
from the canvas, give him new dimension; take him
to the lakeside where he'll run in sunlit leaping, swim
toward the horizon—beside him, his shadows lightly fading.

Good Friday

We always liked an empty church better:
the hollow, the smell, the echo of a cough,

a dropped kneeler in a vacant pew. And you,
reverent-hearted boy, tiptoeing through

the wide aisle, your earnest smile.
No crowd, no prescription for us two.

Those windows golding your shoulders.
You, glowing in rose and blue.

Circuition

I
Seventeen and off work tonight
in Ocean City, Maddie and I step out
on the boards to look for strangers—
they have to be strangers

or it won't work. We find two:
one, a tall drink of water
(as my mother would say)
with black hair and clear eyes

like Diamond's, my Siberian husky
back home in the city. The other, shorter,
blond, whistling through puffed lips—
the kind you want to gorge on.

The boys are leaning on the railing
near the steps to the beach, watching
the advancing black water—closer
now that the sun's gone down—

as it foams under the rising moon,
spills itself over the jetty.
Its crash provides just enough background
to muffle our lame accents

as Maddie and I sidle up to them
and with straight faces, chat
in sophomore French
to get them to look.

II
My daughter coos from her crib,
a delicate diction
in mourning-dove meter.

An instant bilinguist,
I reply
in a thick accent.

III
Monica and I are on a summer trek
through Ireland. In jeans and hiking boots

we climb castle stairs in County Clare
where Celtic queens ruled in armor and gold.

In Dingle, she takes a picture of a cow
who's poked its head through the window

on her side of the car when we stop,
waiting for the gnarled farmer to goad her

from our way. We play here
at gypsies, sisters, faeries, saints.

Now, as we drive back toward town
and dinner, she turns to me, keen:

"Mom, let's talk with Texas accents
at the pub tonight!" She's seventeen.

IV
My granddaughter nudges her way in silence.
Even my daughter makes no sound in labor
—but squeezes our hands and breathes,
her brow the bearer of the tale. The woman
next door screams and I wince, but even her baby
knows birth is a quiet thing, the advance
through the aphotic, narrow space alone, steady
as stone, sure as faith will carry. We ten-count
Monica's breathing, her husband and I, as she abides,
wishes to be finished till, finally, Evelyn crowns
these hours with her close-eyed entrance, reaches
her new-freed arms straight toward her mother
and cries her thanks, shouts her congratulations.

Hail the Horse
    —on viewing *Whistlejacket* by George Stubbs, c. 1762

Hail the gallop-startle of chestnut stallion,
of creamy palomino across a verdant plain;

Hail the mane, the tail, their glory in the wind,
lifting and landing against neck and rump;

Hail the curve of glossy haunches in the noon sun,
the elegant bend of hind-legs-stance, of sleek necks

bent to buttercupped meadow; Hail the hay, manure—
their commingled aroma; Hail the young girls

who worship at the stable, feeding and grooming,
rubbing oil into tack, hoisting their slim selves

to those thousand pounds of power; Hail the equine
force: genesis of Pegasus, centaur, Epona,

of Uffington and unicorn; of mythic gifts: fertility,
protection, salvation; Hail the speed of transport,

of winged thunder, of clip in dust, clop on cobblestone,
mud-suck and whinny, nudge and bridle-bite. Hail all,

Hail all things Horse.

Saturdays

We huddled, my dad and I,
under the turquoise window—
our shoulders bending the gold-bright
slant that bounced from the linoleum
beneath our slippers to spray the room.
Winked at each other
as we spread yellow mustard on squares
of saltines topped with sardines—
separate from the *ughs!* of the others—
there, reserving our adjoining mansions
as we grinned this memory toward heaven.

On Johannes Vermeer's *The Milkmaid*
        —1658

She hangs, wooden-framed, on the kitchen wall, white-capped,
constant, her sturdy hands guiding the stilled milk ribboned
between the lip of her pitcher and the chunky bowl below.

She is dressed as the table is draped, in layers:
royal blue dominant, golden rounds of bosom and bread—
though the table, not the color, is more testament to her truth.

She is tight, tidy, her modesty rosed in full cheeks
above the high-necked, corseted bodice that hides
the woman of her, the buried abandon that might yet stir

with loosened hair, an unlatching from service, a shift
in her viewpoint; a flight into that centuries-steady sunslant
that beckons at this window, lights her ordered profile.

Small Things

It's the small things that grip us in the wake
of sudden death: his soft sigh coaxing
the glued handle back to the rare heirloom cup;
his stretch before rising as he studies the scud
of a cloud framed in the wide window
above the bed—the underside of his blond lashes
directing your gaze. The dust universe that glides
over those sunlit argyles pointed heavenward
from the footrest. The porch lamp's eye winking
welcome beneath a bobbing August branch
as he holds your hand across the cobblestones
of the candled courtyard; the last shoe he tied;
his red comb finally found beneath the cushion
of the vacant La-Z-boy.

The Same Sunset

On summer evenings, my father watched
at the back window after supper, the hot white sky
turn pink, inhaling the clean of mowed grass,
the faint remains of the O'Briens' barbecue
seven backyards away. He yearned to pack us up,

move to somewhere in New England, he said.
Open a General Store. Pen his memoirs—
what he could bear to recall of the war—
the small triumphs, dark laughs, the late-March
trek home in '45. The G.I. Bill had fulfilled one dream.

My mother, another. She'd waited,
writing amusing letters she knew he needed
as she read between the lines of his. Then,
a post-war marriage, a gaggle of noisy children,
mortgage payments—filling his time

in the usual order of things. The cost of love
that tucks private schedules into back pockets
like saved movie stubs—their showing up a season later
evoking again the allure of other lives better scripted.
Lives, though filled with color and dash, are still

those of others. Not the one chosen, with its
day-by-day cultivation, its deep-drilled wells
gushing surprise drives to the beach, the handgrip
trust of a frightened child, a carry-out pizza
when misjudged timing burns the casserole,

and the grit of past-due bills and squabbling kids
that scrape the nerves. My father's life cast him
as uncomplaining supporter, teacher by day, helper
with homework most nights, a weekend musician
(we thought the gigs were just for fun

not the extra income). When he wasn't leading
boy scouts or coaching my brothers' baseball teams,
or presiding over meetings as three-time president
of our high school parents' club, he was rehearsing
new songs with my mother, writing arrangements,

taking her twice a year for weekend getaways.
Working with joy at his life, our life. The last time
I saw him alive, he was waving good-bye to me
from the same window he always watched at—
where the same sun sets over the same tended roses

at the edge of the yard, the familiar angle of sky
shafting into the same room where we all took
our meals, argued our points, blew out hundreds
of birthday candles. Passing the years
                    by the worthy cost of love.

April Buck

He bounds from the woods
sunbreasted, cotton-trotting

across the back field, dipping
and lifting in his hosanna

to the green-lit morning.
His hooves rise from the dew

in dressage moves as he passes
left to right to the limits

of the kitchen window's grasp.
Oh, if I could feel as he feels—

know the muscled swell, the heft
of breath—I'd know his stretch

as it bursts all bounds; his glee
as it knows no compass; his heart

as it partners with the dawn in one
glittering burst of measureless light.

III

Spoil of War

I

You learn your father fought in the war because you listen
from the top of the stairs when the fervid "Young Dems" meet
in your living room Tuesday nights. You gulp the stories
that pour amid the laughter and bottles of Bud and long silences:

"I remember that poor bastard, Pirelli, man—falls off
the back of the tank at Dunkirk, slices his ass
on a jag of stone—gets a damn Purple Heart!"

Whelan chimes, "I got back in March—my mother had kept
the Christmas tree up, lights n' all. No needles left,
but the tinsel still draped—my gifts there waiting on the floor."

Your father adds his tale of bunking night after pungent night
in a soaking foxhole under a tindalo tree in the Pacific—the ping
of beetles bouncing from the helmet he covered his face with.

This is funny every time he tells it, every time you beg him
to tell you more about the war. It's the only story he ever tells.
What's been withheld because you're only five,
because you're only seven, is revealed one Saturday morning

when you're ten, when a forgotten Reader's Digest on the back
of the commode tells of Adolph Eichmann. Frightened, you
ask your father if this is truly true, and he sags to his chair,
stares at you—his answer in the heater's moan, the knocking pipes.

II

What if we could have known them then, seeing,
as though their skin were cellophane,
clear into the light beneath—the shimmer knitted within
the stretched tissue, ragged-mended bones,
flagging hearts. If we could have known
those noisy (or mute) minds that still wondered
as they mustered what was left to them

for the longer march ahead,
as they passed through our postwar childhoods:
the bent Mr. Zielinski, who trudged
from truck to stoop up and down each dawn,
his crooked-knuckled hands lugging milk,
its cream risen in the chill
for slippered customers to spoon to honeyed tea;
the dress man named Marty who pulled up
twice a season in his two-tone Chevy
to haul from the rack across his back seat
a trove of garments to sell
from the arms of Gram's living room chairs;
or old Mrs. Katz with the odd tattoo on her arm
who used to give us a dime
for helping her inside with her groceries—
we'd thank her, smile into her rheumy eyes and,
in some subconscious way, figure she was clueless
about what's important to the young.

There was one, though, who gave us sight:
that widowed white-haired recluse down the block
who walked his schnauzer in the park each night.
The one who raised his T-shirt once
for an *Action News* reporter's interview of locals
during Holocaust Remembrance Week.
Fixed on his worsted couch before tabled family photos,
he shared the Mengele experiment
jagged across his belly. Sighed his pride
in his own sturdy stock, in the blessed path he'd forged;
his gratitude to that long-ago rescuing soldier
whose blurred and noiseless appearance had proved then,
as Pandora in her horror, in need of a balm, discovered—
the last thing indeed *is* hope.

III
The night I knew
I loved you
we sat at a table
in the bar
where we met,
a summer job
at the beach for me—
then my furthest reach.
I studied the evenness
of my fingernails
pressed against
the netted sleeve
of the candle glass
I pushed toward you
to light. Drew in
the damp pine
of the old walls,
the wheeze
of draft beer poured,
the house band's cover
of The Guess Who's
"No Time."
Wondered
if you could come to me,
this place for you
a dangerous womb—
a dark shield
from the time
the place
the reason
they'd pinned
that Silver Star
to your chest.

IV
She discovers she's having a boy and she starts.
She rests her palms on her belly and turns away
from the 6 o'clock News; from her colleague's tale

of a neighbor's son honored last week at Arlington;
from the blue joy brought in by a boy.
She thinks about Thetis, and Mother Mary, her own

mother and grandmother, four of many millions
who've breathed worry in, peace out out; worry in,
peace out. And she watches her son grow: at nine,

building a snow fort with his friends, shouting
each to the other, "Halt, or I'll shoot!" At twelve,
his forearms bulging as he whacks the ball

out of the park, high-fiving his mates to adrenaline hoots.
She studies her nephews, the teenagers at the mall,
the young man bent to a chain of thirty shopping carts,

and she knows the flower-giving, heavy-lifting hearts
that pulse inside their muscled chests, the fears
that prompt their swagger and playground cursing.

And when she's alone, she opens her palms skyward,
closes her eyes. Lifts a prayer to the face of God.
Breathes in hope against the odds.

Bronze Veins
> —*The Three Soldiers*, Viet Nam Memorial, Washington, D.C.

And the stationary eyes, the light-caught
angled folds of jungle fatigues, boot laces—tied
in real time by 18-year-old fingers.

These are what stomach-punch every time. Yes,
the wall impresses with its yards and yards
of names, its dark reflection of the weathered faces

of wheel-chaired, grey-pony-tailed vets,
still weighting bar stools and shrink couches,
tossing through the fearsome nights.

But the statue reminds. The once bell-bottomed,
peace-signing young mother, his child still in her
womb when he died three continents away

today kneels on a cushion to ease her arthritic knees,
her slim shoulders now hunched below a gray bob,
as she searches these still faces yet again.

She comes every year, notes the saplings
that spindled through those months
when it was first unveiled, now sturdy trunks

bearing knotted limbs whose wide flowering
each April shades the two-down-generation visitors
who never knew them—fathers, grandfathers—

only follow the lead of former girls-next-door
now grandmothers, still stunned by those
teen-aged veins in the hand that holds the M16.

The Potato Eaters
> —Vincent van Gogh, 1885

Oh, their great chunks of faces—bulged eyes,
bilging lips; veins worming in hunks of hands
clumped under the dull lamp swagged above them
like a dim-glowing god smearing its oily grin
over all—pungent clothes, mildewed walls.
Brown, more brown, and the deep earth celled
in them as though they too live underground,
thickening in the dark, stationary, waiting
to be plucked from their soiled cradle—
lifted to the crusty table, all cluttered cups
of muddy brew, a common plate of sustenance
hewn from the dirt to which they'll return
none too soon for blessed rest
from this. They make of it the best.

Miscarriage

The morning you left, I lay on a steel bed
in a silvered room—ticking my right thumb

on my right thigh—the minutes clicking
across the face of the relentless clock

that mocked us through a fluorescent fog—
folded myself to the dark heat of my womb

where, blank and barely alive, out of breath
in its frantic search for you, its membranes

at wits' end—its pulse slowed to a numb standstill.
I netted my fingers over my belly then

and blessed you on your way—a meager baptism
to light your fully-formed wings.

On a March Morning

This yellow sheet,
stilled in shake above the bed,
makes such beauty in its lilts
of shade and light—
its breadth bounding left, right
and forward from my hands—

as that delicate quilt of fog
last week on my way to work,
lying low, unstirred
above the waking field,
layered against the early sky:
two geese beneath—she, nesting,
he, guarding—a few yards off the road
amid the wind of rush hour—
their quiet an invitation
to the simplicity of bed-making.

Lesson

Sharon is moving. Not only that,
she doesn't even want to play anymore,
my daughter tells me, at a time
when little girls need best friends.
After supper, we take a walk.
I think of an old Carly Simon album,
one wise song—tell her about Gwen Carter
and how much her friend missed her
once she moved away. We go silent awhile.
She picks some Evening Primrose
from the scrub at the edge
of the field next to our house.

And I suddenly wonder if I'm lying to her—
that Sharon may never think of her
once she's gone, that friendship can thin
the way dew does when its drench
evaporates in the sun, leaving the garden petals
pinched and spent. The way I, at 11, left
Maryellen with brimming eyes in the hallway
that day, our plans dashed against the wall
I'd crafted between us—and I wonder now
if her mother had to do the work of healing
after supper then; had watched like this,
her daughter gather Evening Primrose
along the edge of an abandoned field.

Storm

We are chopping onions
by the kitchen window
when it charges, racing
from the western horizon—
howling, foaming angry—
flinging its turbid curtain
across our evening.
It lunges at the wires strung
from the road; rips them
with a roar, spitting
flares to char the pines,
the grass, shattering
the light to plunge us
to an impulse long
forgotten. Eyes wide
in the dark, we fumble
for candles—flame to douse
our alarm—while our high
registers betray us
as we strive to soothe
worried children who pretend
for our sakes to believe
the beast can be slain.

A Slight Remove
> —for my stepchildren

No, you are not of my womb.

Your father didn't make me your mother
by the natural wend of youthful love and family-building—
you've had that mother love from another. My love for you

comes at a slight remove. Not known in the casual way
that comes through water and blood, knitted into the early seed.
You have taught me that love can bypass native passion,

unfurl slowly by practice, a steady attendance. This love
is sentient at its very beginning. *Decides* to embrace,
to take instruction from ardent intention. Cultivates

an inward climb toward a second life whose richness springs
from struggle—a separate seed gestating underground
through a hard winter, finally releasing into bloom.

A Blight in the Growing Season
—Holicong, summer, 2008

They come, finally, from the South,
after months of rumors,
our catching the notice in the papers:
burly men in Wranglers and hard hats,

lining our road with their Ditch Witches,
Porta-Johns, their Ford and Chevy pickups;
tramping over the field just yards from our home
to make a six-month living far from their own.

Kindly men, we're to find, waving to us
in the sun as we pull in and out of the driveway;
earnest men with families, apologizing
for the intrusion; caught by financial need

in a mission to upturn the green lands
from Texas to New York, displacing the deer,
the fox, the hawk and owl from border to border
to border. On the first day,

their grim machines thunder a campaign
across the unsuspecting glen, green
and blinking with butterflies, while we watch
from the porch, steps from the buried pipeline

—its widening the narrowing of our back yard.
Chill blades shear through the hearts of oak
and birch, cut the dogwood off at the knees,
while mechanical arms like stolid pall bearers

carry the corpses upright to the edge
of the clearing. Toss them
to their unblessed graves. The three-story
pines thud to the earth that shudders

under the blow. And we watch
as their branches quell in the dust; smell
their tangy blood leaking on the breeze
which, newly widowed, goes suddenly mute.

Carried Cups of Tea

With some rubbing alcohol and a paper towel
I wipe away my husband's flu germs: keyboard,
mouse, the veneered edges of the desk. And as I watch
the wet dry, I think of Nina, a month past

sitting shiva. Her husband's fatal cancer. We drove
through sideways rain that night—asphalt shine
challenging our understanding of the road—to offer
homemade applesauce, and bow our Christian heads

during the intermittent Kaddish, reminded
that whatever beyond faith animates—moss, elk,
coral, steam, mouse, man—was ringing through
the overflow of mourners, filling Nina's house.

I caught her eye from across the foyer, my guilt gripping:
husband by my side; miles away, my son driving
to his girlfriend's—not sitting hip to hip with me,
as her son was, on the low couch, her hand flicking

the back of his hair, his spare words husking toward
the uncle rabbi. And now, in my home, the rooms aired,
even the keyboard "safe," I weep again at Nina's loss.
Wonder if she'd clean these keys. Or be grateful

to tap her fingers into her husband's fingerprints,
his quiet virus prompting carried cups of tea,
glasses of clear water to gentle chalky Vitamin Cs,
a tucking in of blankets, a cool hand on the forehead.

On Receiving News of Sudden Death

The initial tears spring
not as the dredging kind
by which the flood glugs up
from the silty layers of the heart
where the thickest reasons live
but as a muted seep—
bound by disbelief—breaking
from just beneath the surface
as a leak wells through a pond's crust
scraped by low-hanging twigs:
a louvered window on the deep.

Stuck in the Thick

You rise each morning in pain—at the knees, the hips,
the brain. That nightmare won't leave even
at the gray light that early grudges down the walls.

Your tossed robe waits on the corner chair for you
to wrap yourself against the dread that, like your shadow,
like the birthmark on your wrist, is always with you.

You take your tea standing at the sink,
watching out the window the green dull,
birdsong barely audible, faded as any notion of joy.

Oh, to stay in bed, swaddled in the warm,
unconscious to the nag. Caressed by the linens
the way no one out here would ever care to hold you—

accepting each curve of arm, of shoulder, of lip.
They always told you to stop feeling sorry for yourself,
but in the deepest moments, who better for the job?

The Leaving

I watch the blue, minute rivers
in your temples swell and fall,
your biceps flex beneath the sleeves
of your *Quicksilver* T-shirt

as you stretch, pushing your shoulders
to the back of the booth,
gathering weight for the next round.
So many good reasons

why it's time to go. I want to say,
"I know, but I wish to explain
why this is so hard for me." But I don't.
Your Sprite glass sweats

to a puddle I refrain from blotting,
sitting on my hands, blinking back
the sting. I know you must leave,
your dreams cresting as they are

to a height wilder than anything
you can tame; know my time is up.
For now. Still, I want to show you
more: how to make a roux,

play the spoons, navigate white caps.
Travel with you on a train
from Paris to Istanbul.
Teach you again how to need me.

Offering Grace
      —for my daughter

Big apron draped over her skirt and blazer,
knee socks puddled above saddle shoes tucked
into the scuffed rungs of the high stool, she perches:
Art class, junior year, her heavy auburn hair.
She leans to the eight-by-ten-inch panel,
her right forefinger shaping a three-petaled daisy
into the wet plaster.

Mother's Day again and still it hangs above
the kitchen shelf, weighty in its light-reflecting white.
Gentle, barely-perceived swells convey her
hand-smoothing of each surface, careful curves
marking her attention—edges of petal from sides
to center. Her invisible prints like held breath
exhaling now into my tracing hands.

Contemplating Constance Charpentier's *Melancholy*
—1801

Her neck bends, folding her shoulders to the burden
that casts her listless gaze downward, emptying
her expression, reflecting the numb of the mind
behind her eyes. Her bountiful figure, swathed in white,
blooms as flowers do from winter's dark, argues
with the black bank of earth that surrounds her,
on which she rests, on which her indigo shawl sprawls
forgotten—as in the way tragedy nulls the senses,
causes a halt in movement, an oblivion to the night-chill,
to hunger, to fatigue, to the onlooker who wonders
at the abandoned public demeanor, the unabashed
succumbing to the mastery of an uninterested universe.
Yet for all her blue, her deep, one hand lies open, fingers
pinked petals, palm allowing the light that singles her out.

Taking Away the Keys

She sits obedient, my mother, turning her head this way,
then that, looking down, then up, handing me bobby pins

as I roll each curl into place. Her white hair is coarse,
harder to tame now than it was back when she did it herself

over the bathroom sink, dipping her narrow comb into
a plastic cup of water to keep from running the tap, raising

the monthly bill. Then, she was in charge of herself and us.
She could give Jimmy Sculley an earful for his incessant teasing

every time he ruined another leafy afternoon for us girls
playing dolls on the porch—send him packing down the street,

chancing looks over his shoulder to make sure she wasn't
chasing him. She could argue down like nobody's business

any merchant on the avenue if she thought the meat was too old,
the peaches too bruised; belt out the kitchen window any old

War-time standard as she rehearsed for my father's Swing band,
embarrassing my sister and me. Now, she trusts my directions,

knows she's not in charge here. Some days she enjoys
the turning over of energy, the freedom of it. Others, she's restless,

longs for her car, her keys—gone back to the dealer. When I was five,
I looked up at her standing at the hall mirror, marveled

at her precision: folding in half one square of toilet tissue to blot
her crimson lips. When she opened it, there was the wide mouth

saying hello, making me giggle to keep from crying as she
placed her beret slightly on the side of her head and shrugged on

her big shoulder bag to go to choir practice Thursday nights. Now,
she looks up at me, asks whether there are cookies after dinner.

Takes her medicine from my hands as I tuck her in.

Thrift Shop

How to resist this slightly worn little number:
V-necked, three-quarter sleeves, perfect shade of gold—
the dry cleaner's red tag pinned in the collar.

Yes, now and again, I grow weary of buying my clothes
second (maybe third?)-hand—everything just a little off
my true size, just a little faded. But—

when a sweater's sleeve features tags from *Bloomie's*,
from *Talbot's*, from *Chico's* to show the original owner
never even wore it...well! How can I turn down

this 93% discount off the original price?
What's this? Everything 2 for 5 bucks! Check out this
pair of black slacks—the legs long enough, for a change,

to compensate for my high waist, the butt just loose enough,
with just shine enough (hey, I can cover that with a long sweater)
to show they've known their share of lounging. How can I

possibly ignore this? There's something communal,
transcendent even, about clothes another has worn, something
big-sister-hand-me-down-familiar, bargain-hunter-Eurekaed about it

that makes the imagined memories of strangers collide,
so that family parties, and the spills of children, and bus trips,
and movie seats, and washings, all tumble together

through a warp of time, folding themselves in a May-December
marriage of humble treasure and glorious frugality.
      Oh, wow! Get a load of this...

Madame X
    —John Singer Sargent, 1884

She appears to be made of cream, poured
cold to an ebony jar. Her shoulders
bubble over a sugared rim. Arms drip down
the sides—drizzles of light stilled in their path
toward a cinnamon base—resolve in generous
drops that cling on one side to a fan at the curve
of the vessel; on the other, to a polished table
that stays the movement, balances the image.
She invites us to salivate, to sip at every
rondure, stir at every thrust of the flask
as each beckons our eye, questions our thirst:
the milky curve of neck, the smooth peaks
of nose, of chin, of pomegranate lips; the dollop
of her tiara. All whipped to a chilly confection.

Still Life on a Buffet

Centered among crystal glasses, one tall candlestick
presides, its curves like one woman standing
on the shoulders of another, its footing felted to keep
its landing gentle. The pewter emits such a muted
sheen the sun, or the moon, or the lamp in the window
all glance off the outward thrusts in shy shining,
not as brass screaming, "See me—I'm so very bright!"
but whispering, "Come, approach, fill me with wax, touch
your flame to the wick, and I'll light your evening with heat,
with dance. My fire will say, 'See, you are not alone
when you know my movement, follow my hula, my cha-cha,
my rhumba; my stretching with the breeze—be it your own
exhalation, the summer curtain's flutter, the passing of a cat,
its eyes green-glowing, reflecting our two lit flames.'"

When Our Guests Have Gone

Tonight
I want to fold
into your deep
once more, sink
into your
heated tent,
your scent
a cedared
luxury. To know
your beard,
silver glinted,
brushing
my skin awake
as its smokey
darkness did
at our beginning.

The rush
of claret pulse.
The lush
of our content
a dram our youth
could never
have drunk.

IV

Mother

When your world shrinks to two rooms of whatever furniture
will fit, your hummel collection, and a drawerful of photos
which you sort and give away in handfuls to whoever cares
enough to visit; when a box of birthday chocolates outlasts

your desire to open it, and the nurses tell you *you-can't-take-
your-afternoon-walk-alone-and-certainly-not-without-your-cane-
anymore*, you may find yourself anticipating the rising moon
outside your single window, pining for its heart-piercing beauty

that lifts you in the same sighing it did the Buddha, and Jesus,
and your mother who taught you to gaze upward, thrill
to the brilliant expanse. And now you hurry to knock on every door
on your side of the hallway, point your fellow residents

to their own private parcel of light. Know in that moment
you *live*, still breathe deeply the fullness of your night.

Bride of Christ

An old woman now, rocking in the Motherhouse,
she waits. Her beads pass through her fingers
like slow-moving boxcars through gnarled tunnels

in the valley of her lap. She stares through milky eyes
out the paned window, ponders the stretch of trees
that weep above ground, bowed by a grey-billowed sky.

What of that distant road bent in the undergrowth.
Of those who trod there, dwelt in its shifting openings,
praying their personal prayers. Might she have borne

more than the world in her own supplications?
How many kisses she missed, exhausting Christmas mornings,
proud graduation days. How many of her thwarted progeny

might have borne the banner of a new generation of believers
to swell the song of praise to the one she chose as Husband,
the One who would have endured without her wearing His ring,

uttering vows in a black wedding dress, thick energy standing alone
at the altar next to an invisible Love. Hers, a meager reception,
a solitary honeymoon, a communion shimmered in veils.

* *The term "bent in the undergrowth" in line seven is drawn from Robert Frost's "The Road Not Taken"*

The Saint of Calcutta

—on a series of paintings by Bruni Sablan:
Tribute to Mother Teresa, 2008

With her thumb, she lifts away
the veil from her brow, allows the boiling
sweat-fall to roll through her eyelashes,
drip from the tip of her nose, pool
in the deep ravines around her mouth.
She looks heavenward for a cheer,
for a nod that notes this is all
worth something; that she didn't
misspend her finished youth. Tonight

she'll dust off her sandals, wash this habit,
hang it to dry, and lie prostrate for rest,
for prayer. Bite back the questions
she'll ask God when she gets there.
Fall to a slugged slumber. For now, though,
she'll lug another dog-licked body to cover,
hold its languid hand, mutter quiet prayers
and know by some hope-driven measure
she gave dignity to at least this one.

Life for the Real Artist
—For Frida

What you know struggles from what
you dream—as Jacob with his dark angel
struggled in the night. You expect the dawn,
the sun's lift, as it's always been. Perhaps
marriage, children, perhaps a safe life. Not
what intrudes: illness, mishap, subtraction
from the whole. When the body, the mind
are bound by chance, left wanting by pieces
of their own absence, only the spirit is left
to command attention. So: paint yourself
in braces. Paint yourself in a thorn necklace.
Paint yourself pierced by nails, by arrows,
your rich blood leaking. But paint your
weeping eyes with well-deep dots of light.

An Artist Becoming

As a child, I see patterns
on the covers of my marble copybooks
and connect the sections to bring out the design
waiting to be. Creatures watch from everywhere:
in the wood grain of the doors in my house,
in the swirled patterns of the Oriental carpet
in my grandmother's living room,
the rainbow-slick oil stains on the asphalt
of our church parking lot.
The sun flashes on a skim of water palmed in a dip
in the playground below my classroom window.
It creates flits of light on the ceiling just above
Sister Rita's head, impels me galaxies away
as her chalk clicks long division
on the blackboard.

When I read, I'm distracted by the silent designs
on a page of text, the white spaces *between*
the print, the mysterious absence of ink
out of which an invisible hand has fashioned portraits.
There are Indian teepees and coiled snakes,
dancers contortioned and sometimes a perfect, tiny circle
O-ing a few lines below the line I am reading. Like a star,
it can be seen only when I look a little aside.
These are living faeries, I think, placed there by God
(because God often plays a trickster).
And I'm told faeries appear only to those who thirst to see.
Sometimes I feel honored to see, sometimes afraid to tell.

On Friday afternoons, we have a class called "Picture Study."
We respond to great works like Millet's *The Gleaners*,
Vermeer's *The Guitar Player*, Batoni's *Madonna and Child*,
Van Gogh's *Wheat Field with Cypresses*.
I stare at the shapes and colors, layers and shadows, imagine
what they smell like, these antique people, the dusty wheat,
the yellow and ermine costume; want to unfurl my wings

in this ochre light. And I wish wish wish every hour at school
were Friday afternoon.

***

I'm in church a lot.
Nuns take us much more often than our parents do. Sunday Mass
is for family. Most other visits are for learning. I like church—
the calm, the smell of candle wax, the quiet light. I spend much of this time
examining the stained glass windows which depict scenes of people I think
must have floated inches above the earth all their lives.
The light around their heads sets them apart from anyone I know.
They hold scrolls and quills, staffs and tools, and some, the Child
—and they are beautiful in their folding robes, smooth faces,
delicate hands. They stand on serpents, hold up and put down swords,
kneel before others they see as holier than they are, women and men
who know something I would like to know. I would like
to stand in these windows with the sun brightening and smoothing me
in my perfect clothes. I come to think God has made these windows,
the way we're told God wrote the Bible—who but He could craft
such elegance?

***

I feel pictures
threading through my pencil to shed themselves onto notebook pages:
beached sailboats, their sail-less masts scraping low-coasting clouds,
or barefooted girls in Maxfield Parrish frocks, their sunny hair
horizontal in the breeze. And I know someone invisible
is helping me make them. I call the invisible one God
because this threading, these pictures, come from some place
so deep in the middle of me or so far outside of me, they can only be
from God who blinks roses into being, speaks in tones that change
with the shape of each stirring leaf. God who animates the cat
stretching in the warm window, and halts the waves on the shore,
as, we learned, He reminded Job.

I come to think not everyone experiences *feeling* the pictures inside.

My little sister likes to sit with our grandmother and learn
to knit, to sew, but not to draw so much. My baby brother
is still learning to tie his shoes, so I can't tell about him
yet. My father is a teacher and likes to talk about things but is busy
with his job and, at night, helping us with homework. My mother
likes to sketch, is good at it, and I wish we had time to talk
about the pictures, to talk about how God makes it happen
inside the pencils, inside me, but parents are busy with work
and children and I think it's hard on them when any one child draws
too much on their time.
My girlfriends don't care about the stained glass saints
or even picture study on Fridays. They pass notes
during religion class and don't look up
when the light changes on the classroom ceiling.
I so wish to know someone else who does.

***

In high school,
I thank God for Art class. My teacher, an old nun
who would have been famous if she hadn't spent her life
behind convent walls, recognizes me, gives me projects, suggests
I enter contests. I sit in the same position for hours sketching,
mixing, brushing color to canvas. Here, I'm neither male nor female,
young nor old, body nor air. I forget to eat. It feels like
trusting a river which has taken me into its rush.
It's ecstasy.

My religion teacher is also old, a priest, a Bible scholar
who welcomes questions and explains big ideas
simply. He discusses literature too, and the weight of words,
their power to move us, and I begin to read differently,
notice how the writers say what they say. I begin to examine
The Lord's Prayer, and other ritual prayers
beyond memorization. Where did they come from?
Who wrote them in these forms? They're metaphorical,
they have internal rhyme, slant rhyme. They convey big ideas
in compact language. They are poetry.

Now I want to write too. About important things like thoughts
and families and feelings and beliefs and paintings. I am restless
to begin, but don't know how to begin. But know
I will some day. I come across a quote in English class: Shakespeare
says in the mouth of Isabella, "Go to your bosom;
knock there, and ask your heart what it doth know."

***

Soon, there's a voice:
It's always the same yet comes from everywhere—teachers, parents,
friends, and even a little from inside me: *you'll need a job;
need to be responsible, make a plan; be with someone; maybe
have children.* And I think about balance. About the river.
And the bank.

***

I go to college.
Study, think a lot. Fight and make up with God again
and again. Travel through strings of states where people say *y'all,
you betcha,* and call soda *pop,* sneakers *tenners.*
Backpack through Europe. Inhale the lorry diesel outside London,
hitchhike over the Autobahn. Stand, gazing up
in gilded cathedrals in Paris, in Vienna. Drink red wine,
smoke *Players,* trade books—Hesse, Huxley, Vonnegut, DeChardin
—with fellow travelers on trains. Fly to Mexico.
Sit in dusty bull rings in San Miguel. Caravan to Canada.
Buy *Hobo* paintings in Montreal. Wonder at all of us—people
everywhere breathing the same air, drinking the same water
as the ancients did, as progeny will, washing along this weaving river
together, drifting out, finding our ways back, all of us students of balance
whether we choose it or not, makers of beauty whether we know it
or not. Receivers and passers-on of wisdom and folly,
love and fear and strength. All of it recorded

in architecture, in arias lilting from second-story windows,
clothesline exhibits in city parks, street dancers and poetry corners
from Tokyo to Dublin to Rio to Agra to Gondar to Melbourne to Boston.

       ***

       And I conclude
that any peace I've known has been in the meeting of God's hand
to mine in creating something. That art is an allowance of light,
a rhythm to listen for, a restlessness embraced.

Make Me Believe

Make me believe
I *can* float inches above the earth,
unfurl illuminated in ochre light
if only in realms where no one but I need see.

Poet Bernadette McBride is also an award-winning artist whose written and visual work has appeared in numerous journals, anthologies, and other print venues across the United States. A former poet laureate of Bucks County, Pennsylvania, she has been honored as a Pushcart Prize nominee, both a finalist and runner-up for the Robert Fraser Prize for Poetry, and as second-place winner of the international Ray Bradbury Writing Award. An adjunct English professor, she has taught writing and literature at colleges in Pennsylvania and New Jersey, including poetry and fiction writing at Temple University. She also conducts creative writing workshops in poetry and fiction writing and on the intersection of writing and visual art in various programs throughout Bucks County. She is director of the monthly poetry reading series at Farley's, an independent bookshop in New Hope, PA, as well as editor of the bi-annual anthology of Farley's poets.

ങ ങ ങ ങ ങ ങ

Made in the USA
San Bernardino, CA
27 December 2018